HarperCollins books may be purchased for educational, business, or sales promotional use. For information please write: Special Markets Department, HarperCollins*Publishers*, 10 East 53rd Street, New York, NY 10022.

First published in 2012 by
Harper Design
An Imprint of HarperCollins*Publishers*
10 East 53rd Street
New York, NY 10022
Tel: (212) 207-7000
Fax: (212) 207-7654
harperdesign@harpercollins.com
www.harpercollins.com

Distributed throughout the world by
HarperCollins*Publishers*
10 East 53rd Street
New York, NY 10022
Fax: (212) 207-7654

Editor and project director:
Josep Mª Minguet

Selection, design, text and art director:
Louis Bou Romero

ISBN: 978-0-06-213342-7

Library of Congress Control Number 2011944071

Printed in China
First Printing, 2012

Page one image:
Stephen Jones for John Galliano
Image courtesy of John Galliano

COUTURE HATS

Louis Bou

HARPER
DESIGN
An Imprint of HarperCollinsPublishers

The Milliners

Foreword

Hats! What an adventure through straw and felt, plastics and paper, hope, and dreams.

In this wonderful book, Louis Bou charts the myriad of talented milliners working around the world today, from America to Spain to Japan to Britain. What unites us all? Of course, the love of our métier, but also a wanderlust of exploration of 3-D forms whether narrative or abstract. A panoply of suggestion in each sweeping brim, each trembling feather, each scented flower. It is never easy to create beauty. As much as millinery is a fabulous art, it is craft too and we all burn the midnight oil making and remaking that damn hat, striving for perfection that looks effortless and elegant, dramatic and sublime.

This book is a tribute to millinery's varied creators, who frequently against sensible advice, somehow became embroiled in couture hats—maybe the most esoteric, but certainly the most exciting and visible of accessories. Never before have so many great names been joined together, which I hope negates that often heard diatribe: "Oh you are a milliner, well people don't wear hats anymore, do they?"

Stephen Jones

This page:
Stephen Jones wearing one of his hats
Photography: Justine

Left page:
Stephen Jones for John Galliano
Image courtesy of John Galliano

PHILIP TREACY

Philip Treacy was born in the Galway village of Ahascragh, West Ireland. The son of a baker and a housewife, he had seven sisters and brothers. He moved to Dublin in the mid-80s to study fashion at the National College of Art & Design, and there he created his first hats to go with outfits he designed. In 1988 he was accepted into the MA fashion design program at the Royal College of Art in London, and in 1989 he took one of his hats to Michael Roberts, fashion editor of *Tatler* magazine, and his style editor, Isabella Blow.

In 1990 Treacy graduated from the Royal College of Art with honors and set up a workshop in the basement of Isabella Blow's house on Elizabeth Street. Blow wore many of Treacy's hats, introduced him to designers such as Valentino and Karl Lagerfeld, as well as fashion editor André Leon Talley of *Vogue*. In 1991 Treacy established Philip Treacy Ltd. From there, his career took off. He went on to win the title of Accessory Designer of the Year at the British Fashion Awards for many years, and in 2006 he was awarded an honorary OBE for services to the British fashion industry by Prince Charles and the Duchess of Cornwall.

Now one of the world's most famous hat designers, Treacy has designed hats for Alexander McQueen, Givenchy, Karl Lagerfeld for Chanel, Valentino, Ralph Lauren, and Donna Karan. His clients include Madonna, Celine Dion, Joan Collins, Goldie Hawn, and Boy George, just to mention a few. He designed Sarah Jessica Parker's hat for the film premiere of *Sex and the City*, hats that were worn in the *Harry Potter* films, and a number of the glorious hats worn at the wedding of Prince William and Kate Middleton.

www.philiptreacy.co.uk

Left page: Photograph by Philip Treacy for *Tatler* magazine. All images courtesy of Philip Treacy unless otherwise indicated.

This page clockwise from top left:
White and black silk hat
Madonna hat in natural straw
Photography: Philippe Kerlo
Illustration by Philip Treacy

Left page:
Philip Treacy haute couture show in Paris

This page clockwise from top left:
Hand blocked mini beano headpiece
Sweeping dome in sinamay hat
Hand blocked gondola shape hat
Hand blocked couture boat shape hat
Photography: Philippe Kerlo

This page:
Swirly bow in lurex sinamay headpiece
Photography: Philippe Kerlo

This page:
Philip Treacy and his muse, Isabella Blow
Photography: Kevin Davies

Right page:
Philip Treacy in his studio
Photography: Kevin Davies

This page:
Illustration by Philip Treacy

Left page:
La Dame Bleue headpiece
Philip Treacy for Alexander McQueen
Photography: Catwalking

On these pages:
Philip Treacy hat for Givenchy Haute Couture by Riccardo Tisci
Spring/Summer 2011
Model: Jiang Xiao Yi at Silent
Photography: Kristine Thiemann
Images courtesy of Givenchy Haute Couture by Riccardo Tisci

On these pages:
Philip Treacy haute couture show in Paris
Illustration by Philip Treacy

On these pages:
Philip Treacy for Armani Privé
Images courtesy of Armani Privé

This page:
Photographs by Philip Treacy for *Vogue Gioiello*
Illustration by Philip Treacy

Left page:
Philip Treacy haute couture show in Paris

TOUR DE FORCE

Tour de Force was founded in 2009 by Central Saint Martins's graduate Camille Roman. It was born out of a love of sculptural and innovative details, and a desire to challenge traditional visual associations. The label creates sumptuous luxury looks, taking inspiration from innovative product design concepts, sculpture, and the combination of futuristic aesthetic ideas and whimsy with lush materials and intricate details.

Since its launch, the London-based label has become a favorite of celebrities and stylists around the world, and has been shot by renowned photographers, such as Mario Testino and Tim Walker. Tour de Force regularly creates headpieces for music videos and magazines like *Vogue*, *Tatler,* and *Harper's Bazaar*. Its hats are presented twice a year at fashion week alongside the Tour de Force womenswear collections.

www.letourdeforce.com

Left page: Floral earmuffin headpiece photograph by Robert Harper. All images courtesy of Tour de Force.

On these pages:
Lovestruck headpiece
Photography: Robert Harper
Illustration by Camille Roman

On these pages:
Zig-Zag headpiece
Photography: Robert Harper
Illustration by Camille Roman

This page:
Struck-eye headpiece
Photography: Robert Harper

Left page:
Frolick rose headpiece
Photography: Robert Harper

This page:
Bardot bow hat
Photography: I Heart Studios

Right page:
Jingle cap
Photography: I Heart Studios

This page:
Dressage headpiece
Photography: Robert Harper

Left page:
Flame feather headpiece
Photography: Robert Harper

PINKHAM MILLINERY

Dayna Pinkham began her millinery career in 1982 in Seattle, Washington, where she apprenticed to John Eaton, a venerable milliner and fashion designer. During four years with Eaton, she learned the time-honored methods of design conception, steaming, shaping felt, straw, and buckram over wood blocks, and finishing with fine hand-stitching. In the following years, Pinkham immersed herself in perfecting her craft, studying the history of millinery, and honing her signature style, which mixes the elegance of eras past with clean, modern lines.

Today, Pinkham designs and constructs her hats in her Portland, Oregon, studio, and is renowned as one of the West Coast's top milliners. Her growing national and international clientele includes rock stars, actors, and celebrity athletes. Her custom wedding hats have graced ceremonies across the US and throughout Europe, and her lofty chapeaus have made appearances at Great Britain's Royal Ascot and Newmarket horse races, and in the states at the Baltimore Preakness and Kentucky Derby.

Currently, Pinkham is busy creating her original hat designs with the aid of her own unique block makers. She gives lecture demonstrations on millinery techniques and millinery history to various institutions, including grammar schools, colleges, and historical societies. She plans to continue pushing the hat-making industry out of the past and into the future.

www.pinkhammillinery.com

Left page: Charmeuse floral headpiece photograph by Minh Tran. All images courtesy of Pinkham Millinery.

This page:
Flapper cloche hat
Photography: Minh Tran
Illustration by Dayna Pinkham

Right page:
Coque explosion hat
Photography: Minh Tran

This page:
Pheasant perch headpiece
Photography: Minh Tran

Right page:
Ochre perch hat with ostrich sweep
Photography: Minh Tran

This page:
Dayna Pinkham in her atelier
Photography: Carlin Sundell
Illustration by Dayna Pinkham

Right page:
Winged perch headpiece
Photography: Minh Tran

This page top image:
Hand-blocked straw fedora
Bottom image:
Fur felt homburg
Photography: Carlin Sundell

Right page:
Ostrich lotus headpiece
Photography: Minh Tran

MANUEL ALBARRAN

Manuel Albarran was born in Úbeda in the Spanish province of Jaén in 1968. At age fourteen, he moved to Barcelona to study fashion, and after finishing his studies, he began a career as a multimedia artist. He has worked on a range of different types of exhibitions and collaborated with a number of different types of artists in cities around the world. His portfolio of work includes publicity and advertising campaigns, such as the one for Lavazza's famous calendar and one for Givenchy, cinematic work, and video art. He is also highly respected for his work with metal art, and is well-known in the international fetish scene for creating amazing corsets, lingerie, and jewelry.

Albarran describes himself as an independent and multidisciplinary artist who in recent years has decided to focus his career on designing a new artistic concept, metal couture. For Albarran, this is the careful combination of metal with other highly styled materials to create a futuristic look that is sophisticated, sensual, and alluring. His designs are widely used in the worlds of fashion, art, and cinema.

The celebrities, actors, and musicians who have worked with Albarran include Rihanna, The Black Eyed Peas, Lady Gaga, Tyra Banks, Milla Jovovich, and Zoë Saldana. Albarran also designed all the headpieces and accessories worn by Madonna's dancers during their performance at the 2012 Super Bowl.

www.manuelalbarran.com

Left page: Photograph of Amanda Lepore by Gustavo López Mañas. All images courtesy of Manuel Albarran.

On these pages:
Photographs of Polly Fey by Ginger Studio BCN

On these pages:
Photographs of Bimba Bosé by Gorka Postigo

On these pages:
Photography: Óscar Correcher

On these pages:
Photography: Luz Jiménez-Momediano

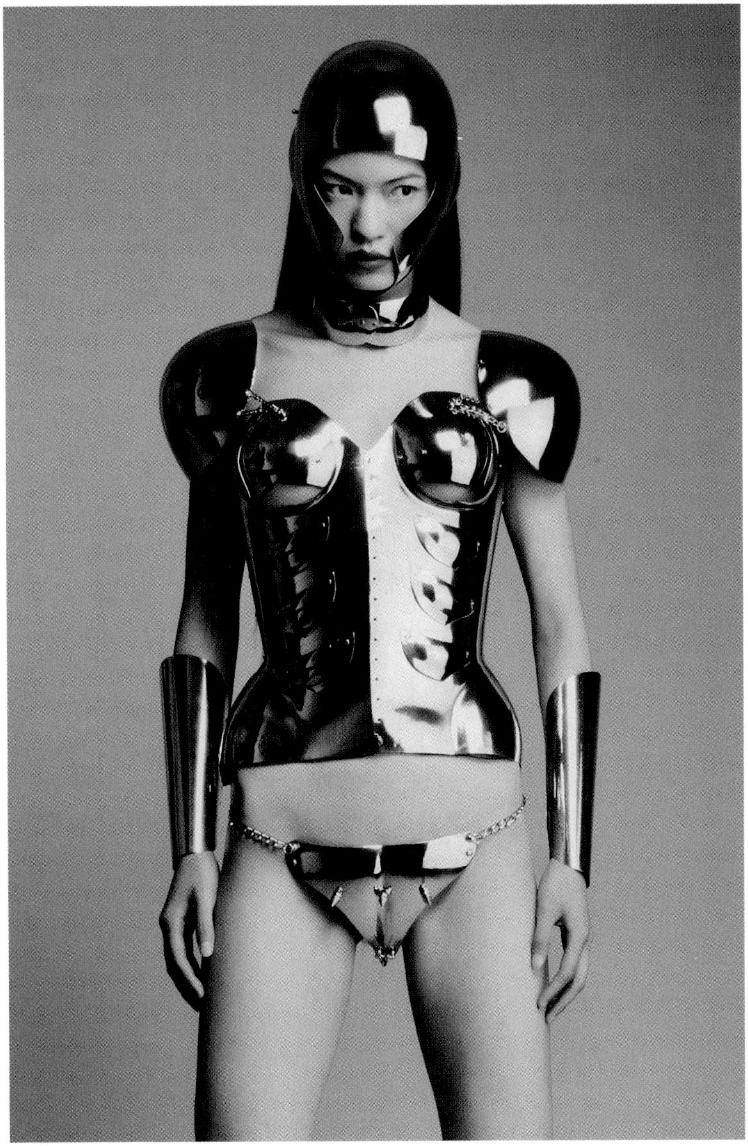

On these pages:
Photography: Mathieu Vladimir Alliard

This page top:
Photograph of Laura Sánchez by Álvaro Villarrubia
Bottom:
Illustration by Ángel Amor
Photography: Álvaro Villarrubia

Right page:
Photograph of Polly Fey by Gustavo López Mañas

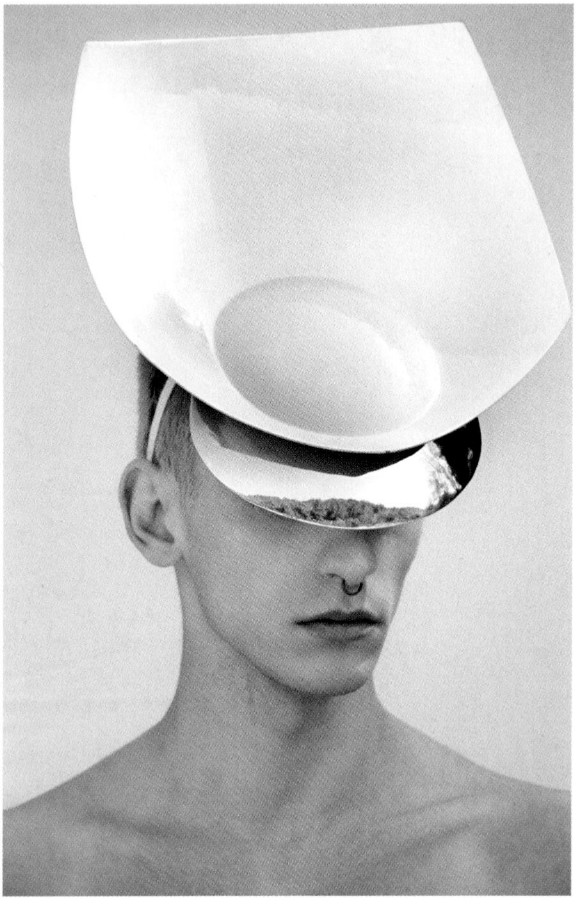

On these pages:
Photography: Gustavo López Mañas

EDWINA IBBOTSON

Edwina Ibbotson first studied millinery at the Fashion Institute of Technology in New York with legendary hat designer Ann Albrizio, and then at the London College of Fashion with Marie O'Regan, a favorite designer of Queen Elizabeth II, while working for top London milliner Philip Somerville. Her weekends were spent taking classes with milliner Rose Cory on Saturdays, and on Sundays with a French milliner, Rolande Bouget.

Ibbotson has now worked in the millinery world for more than twenty years. Her designs are feminine and elegant, and include chic beaded headdresses, delicate soft tulle and floral designs, demure feather headpieces, and beautifully designed veils and hats for the modern bride, stylish mother of the bride, and wedding guests, as well as for other social occasions.

Using a modern take on traditional millinery techniques, Ibbotson's signature look is flirtatious, timeless, and romantic with a vintage feel. Her clients visit her at her London studio, and she collaborates with them to physically create the hats they've dreamt up. Her work can also be purchased from her online store.

www.edwinaibbotsonmillinery.com

Left page: Ascot hat photograph by Claudine Sinnett. All images courtesy of Edwina Ibbotson.

This page:
Pink flower candy hat
Photography: Claudine Sinnett

Right page:
Black and white cocktail hat
Photography: Claudine Sinnett

This page left to right:
Beaded top hat
Gold mesh sinamay hat
Photography: Simon Tomkinson

Left page:
Ascot hat
Photography: Joanne Aldridge

This page clockwise from top left:
Pink silk cocktail hat
Red fur and felt beret
Leopard straw cocktail hat
Beaded disc cocktail hat
Illustration by Edwina Ibbotson

Right page:
Leopard cocktail hat
Photography: Claudine Sinnett

HOUSE OF FLORA

Flora McLean is the head designer of fashion label House of Flora. Inspired initially by Claude Montana, Pierre Cardin, and André Courrèges to study fashion design, McLean earned an MA in Fashion Womenswear at the Royal College of Art prior to establishing the House of Flora label. As the line has grown, so has McLean's name, and in 2010 she was selected to take part in the prestigious Jerwood Contemporary Makers exhibition.

House of Flora specializes in avant-garde headwear for the catwalk, fashion campaigns, and independent collectors. The unique appearance of House of Flora headwear is driven by the materials used to create it: PVC, Perspex, felt, leather, wood veneer, and nylon. It is influenced by geometry, historical figures, and modern art.

The success of House of Flora's hats, has allowed McLean to expand the line to include a commercial range of fashion jewelry and eyewear, and different types of her creations have been worn by celebrities, such as Kate Moss for *Vogue Paris*, Amber Rose, Paloma Faith, Kelis, and Helena Bonham Carter, as well as photographed by the likes of Paolo Roversi, Nick Knight, and Arthur Elgort. The label has collaborated with fashion designers, such as Matthew Williamson, Blumarine, Rocco Barocco, Diane von Furstenberg, Katharine Hamnett, Amy Molyneaux and Percy Parker for their PPQ fashion line, Bruce Oldfield, and Riccardo Tisci at Givenchy Haute Couture. McLean also has an ongoing collaborative project with top hairstylist Neil Moodie, and the two have created 'Iconic Heads,' hairstyle hats made in felt and other fabrics.

www.houseofflora.net

Left page: Photograph by William Selden. All images courtesy of House of Flora unless otherwise indicated.

This page:
Rykiel iconic head headpiece
Photography: Lee Broomfield

Left page:
Kelis iconic head headpiece
Photography: Lee Broomfield

This page:
Millinery in Motion runway event
Victoria and Albert Museum
Photography: Lee Broomfield

Right page:
Marcel iconic head headpiece
Photography: Derek John

This page clockwise from top left:
Beyoncé iconic head headpiece
Morrissey iconic head headpiece
Five point iconic head headpiece
Grace Jones iconic head headpiece
Photography: Lee Broomfield

Left page:
Oakey iconic head headpiece
Photography: Lee Broomfield

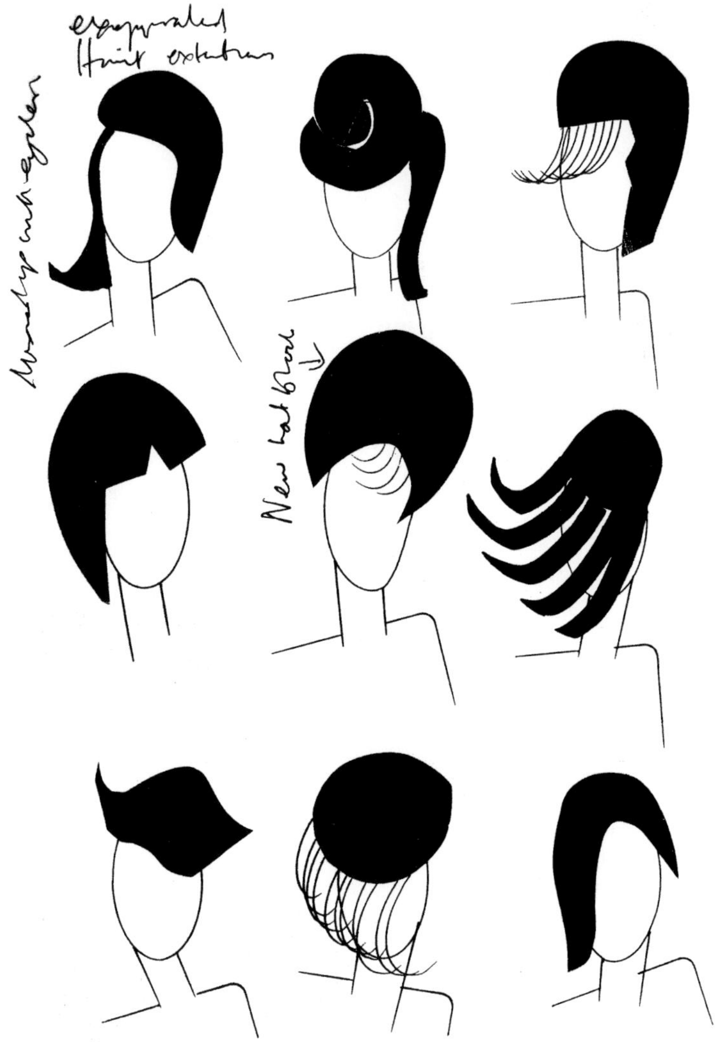

This page:
Illustrations by Flora McLean

Left page:
Elvis iconic head headpiece
Photography: William Selden

On these pages:
House of Flora hats designed for
Givenchy Haute Couture by Riccardo Tisci
Spring/Summer 2010
Photography: Gerard Uferas
Models: Kristy Kaurova at Major and Joan Smalls at IMG
Images courtesy of Givenchy Haute Couture by Riccardo Tisci

This page:
Catwoman iconic head headpiece
Photography: Lee Broomfield

Right page:
Tick iconic head headpiece
Photography: Lee Broomfield

ÀNGEL COLL

Àngel Coll was born in Barcelona in the eighties. He studied at the Academia Internacional de la Moda and the Felicidad Duce College of Design where he specialized in corsetry. After finishing his studies, he presented his first collections at events for young designers. Then, eager to continue growing at a technical level, Coll moved to London where he worked under the distinguished fashion designer Giles Deacon, and revealed his proclivities toward the world of haute couture. When he felt it was time to bring his London adventure to a close, he returned to Barcelona and continued to evolve as a professional, working for the fashion company Custo Barcelona. He also began accepting commissions to make costumes for events and private parties.

In 2010, Coll began developing his own couture label, designing his first and very limited collection of dresses and handmade hats in his small studio in the Gothic sector of Barcelona. Coll is a lover of tailored clothing and lingerie, daring pieces, classic tailoring, and hand-embroidered garments. Dark at times, playful at times, erotic at times, his work defies fashion stereotypes and traditional design rules.

www.angelcoll.tumblr.com

Left page: L'Aragnée hat photograph by Mista Studio. All images courtesy of Àngell Coll.

This page:
Nur Nicht Aus Liebe Weinen hat
Photography: Mista Studio

Left page:
La Vídua Negra hat
Photography: Mista Studio

This page:
The Holy Erzsébet headpiece
Photography: Mista Studio

Right page:
Czarna Madonna headpiece
Photography: Mista Studio

This page:
Dance Like Fred Astaire! headpiece
Photography: Mista Studio

Right page:
The Sacred Hat
Illustration by Àngel Coll

This page:
Mademoiselle Z hat
Photography: Mista Studio

Right page:
Zarah Leander hat
Illustration by Àngel Coll

HEATHER HUEY

A native New Yorker, Heather Huey graduated from Fordham University with degrees in architecture and art history in 2002. She went on to study millinery at the Fashion Institute of Technology before starting her eponymous design label, and later being afforded the opportunity to create her own pop-up installation at HL23 under the Highline Park in New York City.

Huey's line now includes jewelry, but the heart of it is her signature headpieces, which have been requested by stylists Karl Templer, Patti Wilson, Nicola Formichetti, Camilla Nickerson, Lori Goldstein, Ludivine Poiblanc, Giovanna Battaglia, Robbie Spencer, Tabitha Simmons, and Tonne Goodman. She has collaborated with Thakoon, Simon Spurr, Siki Im, and Christian Siriano for New York Fashion Week. And her designs have been photographed by Steven Meisel, Miles Aldridge, and Steven Klein for *Vogue Italia,* Mario Sorrenti and Jean-Baptiste Mondino for *W*, Mert & Marcus for *Interview*, Mariano Vivanco for *Vogue Hommes Japan*, Mario Testino for *V Magazine*, Greg Kadel and Miguel Reveriego for *Numéro France*, Ellen von Unwerth for *VMan*, Terry Richardson for *Purple Fashion*, and Tom Munro for *Harper's Bazaar* and *Vogue Italia*.

www.heatherhuey.com

Left page: Appaloosa hat photograph by Billy Kidd. All images courtesy of Heather Huey.

This page:
Curves Project
Illustrations by Bill Donovan

Right page:
Cocoon Project hat
Photography: Steven Chu

On these pages:
Appaloosa hats
Photography: Billy Kidd

On these pages:
Curves Project
Photography: Steven Chu

GUSTAVO ADOLFO TARI

Gustavo Adolfo Tari was born in Torrellano, Spain. The son of a dressmaker, Tari grew up playing with the fabrics, threads, and needles in his mother's workshop, and became interested in fashion at an early age. In school, he studied hairdressing, a profession he practiced while making clothes with his sister for theater companies. In the late nineties he moved to Barcelona to pursue his real dream of working in fashion, and studied at the International School of Fashion.

In Barcelona, Tari began making headpieces for fashion and advertising. Some of his early headpieces were for the famous hairdresser and stylist Llongueras and for brands such as Volvo. His clothing collections also paraded into the circuits of the art world at museums such as the Museum of Contemporary Art in Barcelona, and the Contemporary Culture Center in Barcelona.

In 2000 Tari legally registered his line of clothing and accessories. Today he is commissioned as a tailor for theaters such as the Liceu and the National Theatre of Catalonia, but most of his time is spent creating custom-made garments, hats, and headpieces, and renting out his extensive collection of vintage clothing to theaters, artists, advertising agencies, and music videos makers, including pop stars such as Madonna and Lady Gaga. In the process of this, his work has been featured in magazines such as *Vanidad*, *Harper's Bazaar España*, *Metal*, and *Neo2*.

www.gustavoadolfotari.com

Left page: Feather headpiece photograph by Manu León. All images courtesy of Gustavo Adolfo Tari.

This page:
Photography: Alicia Calle

Right page:
Crown made of vintage clothing
Photography: Manu León

This page:
Colored tulle headpiece
Photography: Alicia Calle

Right page:
Lace and wire headpiece
Photography: Manu León

This page:
Napoleonic hat embroidered with sequins
Photography: Manu León

Right page:
Hat-mask made with feathers and velvet
Photography: Rebeca Saray,
Jose Valle, and Sergi Devcia

STEPHEN JONES

Born in Cheshire, England, and schooled in Liverpool, Stephen Jones burst into the London fashion scene during its explosion of street style in the late seventies. By day he was a student at Central Saint Martins College of Art and Design; after dark he was one of the era's uncompromising style blazers at the legendary Blitz nightclub—always exquisitely dressed and crowned with a striking hat of his own idiosyncratic design. By 1980, Jones had opened his first millinery salon in the heart of London's Covent Garden. Everybody, from rock stars to royalty, from Boy George to Diana, Princess of Wales, identified Jones as the milliner who would help them make arresting headlines. Jones made millinery seem modern and compelling.

Today, Jones's era-defining edge continues to attract a celebrity clientele, which includes Kylie Minogue, Madonna, Mick Jagger, and Dita Von Teese. He has worked with a wealth of designers from Vivienne Westwood, Claude Montana, Thierry Mugler, and Jean Paul Gaultier throughout the eighties to his current work with Giles, Marc Jacobs, Rei Kawakubo, and Christian Dior Haute Couture. Jones's hats have been an integral component in some of the most memorable runway shows of the past thirty years.

In May 2009, Jones curated a major exhibition at the Victoria and Albert Museum in London, titled "Hats: An Anthology by Stephen Jones." The exhibition opened to huge critical acclaim, receiving over 100,000 visitors, and has since exhibited in Australia and the US. In recognition of his achievements, Jones was named a Royal Designer by the Royal Society for the Encouragement of Arts, Manufactures and Commerce, and awarded an Order of the British Empire by Queen Elizabeth II.

www.stephenjonesmillinery.com

Left page: Photograph courtesy of Christian Dior Haute Couture.
All other images courtesy of Stephen Jones unless otherwise noted.

This page clockwise from top left:
Spirits drifting headpiece
Aftermath 1946 hat
Little fishes headpiece
New horizons headpiece
Photography: P. Ashworth

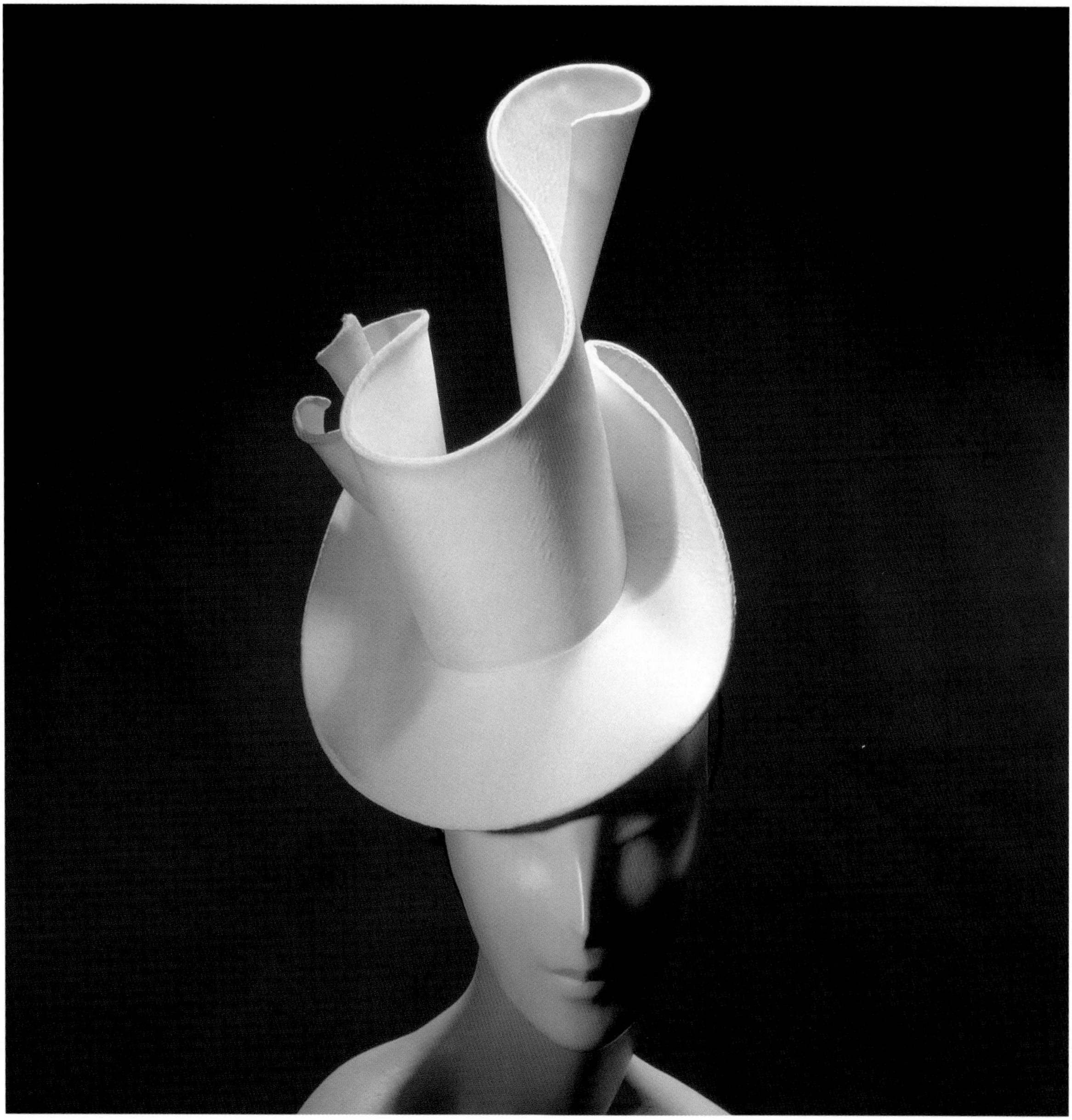

This page:
The water is wide hat
Photography: P. Ashworth

This page:
Stephen Jones hat for
Christian Dior Haute Couture

Left page:
Stephen Jones hat for Giles
Photograph courtesy of Giles

This page:
Stephen Jones hat for
Christian Dior Haute Couture

Right page:
Stephen Jones headpieces for
Christian Dior Haute Couture

This page:
The distraught infanta headpiece
Photography: P. Ashworth
Illustration by Stephen Jones

Right page:
Virgin crown
Stephen Jones headpiece for
Christian Dior Haute Couture

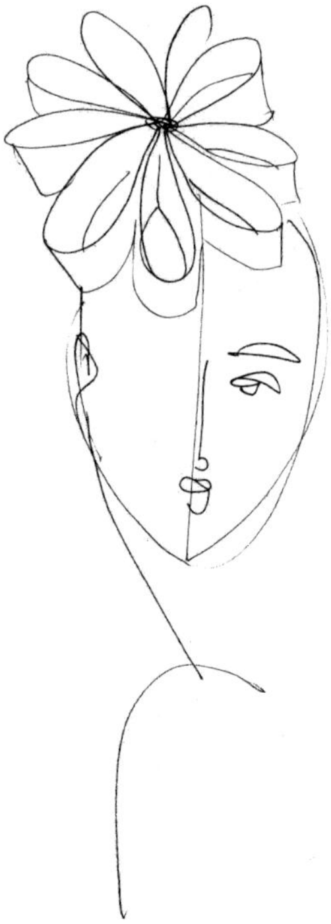

On these pages:
Stephen Jones headpieces for
Christian Dior Haute Couture

On these pages:
Stephen Jones headpieces for Giles
Photographs courtesy of Giles

This page:
Stephen Jones hat for
Christian Dior Haute Couture
Triple vision hat illustration by Stephen Jones

Right page:
Stephen Jones hat for John Galliano
Photograph courtesy of John Galliano

Galliano
Letters
Gossip
Woodie's
Wardrobe
Style section
"Go-Go"
A hand bag!

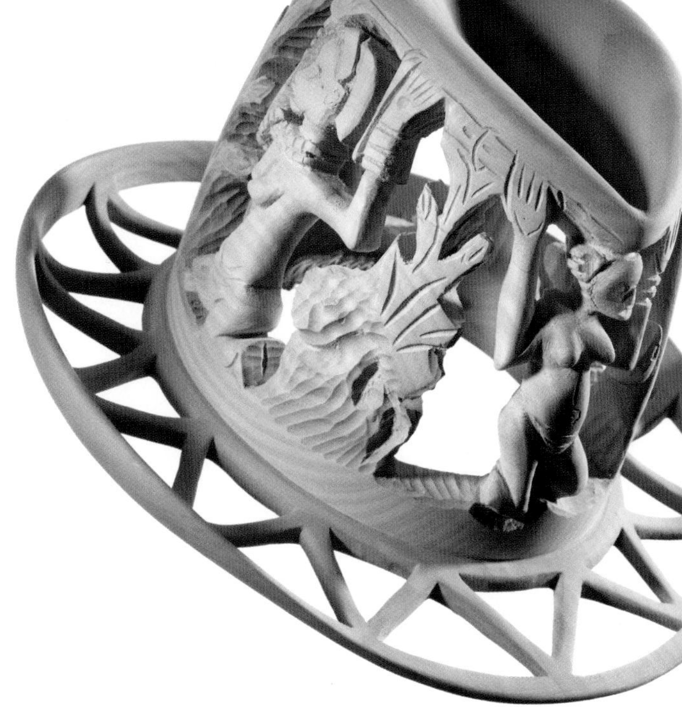

This page:
Chapeau Rita
Photography: Laziz Hamani

Left page:
Stephen Jones hat for John Galliano
Photography courtesy of John Galliano

CHARLIE LE MINDU

Born in Bergerac, France, Charlie Le Mindu was a hairstyling prodigy, cutting and styling hair from the age of thirteen and then going on to study at Formul'a, a French hairdressing academy. Ascending quickly to become a fashionable hair stylist in Berlin, Le Mindu established himself as resident hairdresser at nightclubs such as White Trash, RIO Club, and Barbie Deinhoff. He performed "Live Cuts" in his suite at countless private parties and set up several ensuite salons. He cultivated his own technique and style, and his creations ranged from classic to trashy, refined to over the top.

From Berlin, Le Mindu moved to London where he set up hairdressing residencies in his East London flat and in a number of the city's nightspots. His regular clientele grew to include celebrities like the B52s, Peaches, and Jodie Harsh. His inspiration came from animals and wildlife, and local East London personalities like Slayer and John Waters.

After being featured in *Vogue* and *Elle*, and being selected in 2008 as the *Observer*'s 22nd coolest person in their 'Who's Cool Now' list, Le Mindu decided to take hairstyling to the next level. In February 2009, he launched his first wig collection at London Fashion Week. Since then, the Master of Haute-Coiffure has created many more collections that include both wigs and hats, and he has been featured in publications, such as *Vogue Italy*, *Vogue Hommes Japan*, *i-D*, and *The Guardian*. His clients includes the likes of Lady Gaga and Ayumi Hamasaki, and his work has been exhibited at the Victoria and Albert Museum in London and the Art Athina Fair in Greece.

www.charlielemindu.com

Left page: Photograph by Francisco Gómez de Villaboa. All images courtesy of Charlie Le Mindu.

Left page:
Photography: César Segarra

Right page top image:
Photography: Billa Baldwin
Bottom image:
Photography: Manu Valcarce

On these pages:
Photography: César Segarra

This page:
Photography: Billa Baldwin
Illustration by Charlie Le Mindu

Left page:
Photography: Manu Valcarce

This page:
Photography: Tom Vandepulte
Illustration by Charlie Le Mindu

Right page:
Photograph of Rossy de Palma by Roger Dean

DINU BODICIU

Dinu Bodiciu is a Romanian born, London based, fashion designer. In 2011 he received a master's degree in Fashion Design and Technology at London College of Fashion. His graduation collection, shown at the Victoria and Albert Museum, drew media attention with its shapes, textures, and styling.

Informed by his work experience in theater, Bodiciu's practice is an exploration of the human body, its shapes and particularities. He creates designs that play with volumes, organic textures, and visceral colors in order to alter our perception of the human body. Part of his unique skill set results from his passion for bookbinding, which has informed his deep understanding of fabrics and textures.

Bodiciu's biggest celebrity moment came when Lady Gaga wore one of his designs on *The Tonight Show with Jay Leno*, but his work has also been showcased in established fashion magazines, such as *Vogue Japan*, *Vision China*, *Elle Romania*, and *L'Officiel Ukraine*. His Spring/Summer 2012 collection, Madame De, in an exhibition on display in the Romanian Cultural Institute of London.

www.dinubodiciu.com

Left page: Saturn headpiece potograph by Pearly. All images courtesy of Dinu Bodiciu.

This page:
The Queen headpiece
Photography: Pearly

Left page:
The Moon headpiece
Photography: Pearly

On these pages:
The Silence headpiece
Photography: Pearly

ELLEN CHRISTINE

With more than 30 years of experience designing and fabricating *à la main* millinery, Ellen Christine is well known by fashion editors and the most prestigious stylists. She was born in the 1950's, the decade of Marilyn Monroe and Elvis, an era of percolating pop culture, and was greatly influenced by this. At an early age, she began working in the theater world as a costumer and this gave her a deep appreciation for hats as an accessory. Later, it was advice from Yvonne Deslandres, director of the French Center for Costume Studies, that led Christine to a doctoral program at NYU where she studied costumes and costume history. And since then, New York City has been her base of operations.

Christine oversees her Soho showroom and three New York City studios that produce each of her hats according to her exact specifications. The results reveal her exquisite talent in patternmaking and the use of opulent materials.

Christine's credits include having had her hats in *Vogue, W* magazine, and films such as *Sex and the City 2* and *Cold Mountain*. Her celebrity clientele includes Beyoncé and Beyoncé mother, Tina Knowles, Mary-Kate and Ashley Olsen, Debby Harry, Alicia Keys, Penélope Cruz, Ivanka Trump, Grace Coddington, and Paulina Porizkova. Today, with wholesale as her new interest, Christine hopes to foment the art of hat-wearing across a global market.

www.ellenchristine.com

Left page: Headpiece for Malan Breton photograph by Sandy Ramirez. All images courtesy of Ellen Christine.

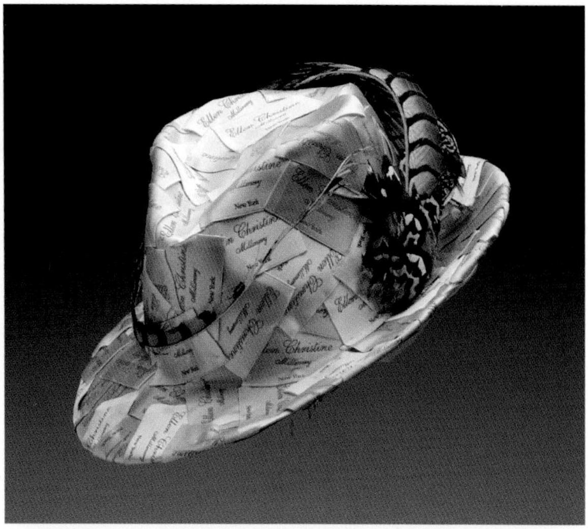

This page clockwise from top left:
Hedy hat
Signature hat
Blue hat
Moët hat
Photography: Tom Bloom

Left page:
Frank Gehry headpiece
Photography: Tom Bloom

This page:
Ellen Christine in her studio
Photography: Sandy Ramirez

Left page:
Photography: Sandy Ramirez

This page:
Hat for United Bamboo
Photography: Casey Showalter

Left page:
Hat for Malan Breton
Photography: Casey Showalter

ANYA CALIENDO

Anya Caliendo was born in Russia in 1974. She inherited her love of hats from her grandmother and her mother, but her first introduction to the world of divine hats happened in the private library of her grandfather. There, at age of three, she discovered a book of photographs of the Russian Royal Family. She was mesmerized by the beauty of the hats worn by Empress Alexandra Feodorovna Romanova and her daughters.

At age 24, Caliendo crossed the Atlantic Ocean and landed in New York in search of the American dream. New York was unexplored territory for her, and she fell in love with the fashion world it gave her access to. She discovered books on two great ladies of millinery, Lilly Daché and Elsa Schiaparelli, and then spent time in London studying under milliner Rose Cory and apprenticing for Stephen Jones in his London atelier. While in London, Caliendo worked with designers and labels, such as Jason Wu, Donna Karan, Kinder Aggugini, Comme des Garçons, and John Galliano. These extraordinary experiences shaped her philosophy, approach, and vision as a milliner.

Caliendo now owns and operates her own atelier. She is in a constant state of production and frequently displays her collections in Paris during fashion weeks. She also continues to collaborate with other members of the fashion world. Caliendo says that the "true enchantment of a woman begins with a fabulous hat, and when crafted by the hand of a skilled milliner, it becomes a natural extension of effortless elegance, a timeless treasure, an *objet d'art*."

www.anyacaliendo.com

Left page: Jardin Des Tuileries hat photograph by Ed Hafizov. All images courtesy of Anya Caliendo.

This page top image:
A thousand and one nights hat
Bottom image:
Rouge Noir hat
Illustrations by Leonid Gurevich

Right page clockwise from top left:
Sweet Memories headpiece
Moulin Rouge. Being in love with Tolouse Lautrec hat
Emerald serpent headpiece
A thousand and one nights hat
Photography: Ed Hafizov

This page top image:
C'est Libertine. Égoïste hat
Bottom image:
Lady Gaga hat
Photography: Ed Hafizov

Right page:
Anya Caliendo's atelier
Photography: Zorz Studio

HATS ARE FRAGILE CREATURES.
PLEASE DO NOT HANDLE THEM!
ASK FOR ASSISTANCE.
THANK YOU.

HSBC
maxell

TOLENTINO

Felipe Vivas, one of the founders of Tolentino Haute Hats, was born in Cáceres, Spain, and grew up with a love of fashion and art developed during a childhood spent in his family's couture ateliers. In the '80s, he moved to Seville where he earned a degree in Fine Arts and met Manuel Carrión, who would become his inseparable companion and his right hand in all of his activities. The duo shared a passion for fashion and began taking millinery classes in Madrid and Paris, and shortly thereafter, they set up the brand Tolentino Haute Hats in Seville. They chose this brand name as a tribute to Vivas's grandfather, an Italian tailor from Tolentino.

Over time, Vivas and Carrión became well-known in the nightclub scene, and word began to spread that they had established a couture hat line. With the support of friends and local institutions, they did their first runway shows. The shows captivated critics and fashionistas.

The fusion of styles of Vivas, who loves bizarre oddities and the underground scene, and Carrión, who is more conservative and elegant, forms a neomodern, yet harmonious, tandem. Their designs are well received by an audience eager for innovation, and their collaborations with other designers have provided them with a rich global perspective on fashion, which shapes their designs.

www.tolentinohautehats.es

Left page: Love Chili headpiece for *45 Magazine* photograph by by Héctor Pérez. All images courtesy of Tolentino.

This page:
Icnic headpiece
Photography: Juan Delgado

Right page:
Cinetic art headpiece
Photography: Juan Delgado

This page:
Photograph of Cristina Ibarra by Juan Delgado

Left page top row:
Moda de Sevilla fashion show
Photography: Chema Soler
Bottom row:
Andalucía de Moda fashion show
Photography: Chema Soler

On these pages:
Pink ball headpiece
Andalucía de Moda fashion show
Photography: Chema Soler
Illustration by Felipe Vives

This page:
La Reina de la Noche headpiece
Photography: Dominik Valvo

Left page:
Andalucía de Moda fashion show
Photography: Chema Soler

This page:
Metropol hat
Photography: Dominik Valvo

Right page clockwise from top left:
Evavila headpiece
Anna headpiece
Pilara headpiece
Animal print headpiece
Photography: Dominik Valvo

This page top image:
Felipe Vivas in his studio
Bottom image:
Felipe Vivas and Manuel Carrión
with Eva and Sara Ávila
wearing Tolentino's hats
Photography: Juan Delgado

Left page:
Nouveau hat
Photography: Dominik Valvo

PIERS ATKINSON

Piers Atkinson has worn nearly as many hats as he's made. Artist, illustrator, milliner, costume designer, party organizer, fashion editor, and fashion journalist–his creative energies are only matched by an insatiable curiosity. He grew up in Norfolk, England, with three generations of women–his mother, herself a milliner, his sister, Lucy, the long-suffering photographic model for his teenage reconstructions of Grace Jones and Art of Noise record covers, and his grandmother, the artist, writer, horticulturalist, and illustrator, Lesley Gordon, from whom he took his multi-disciplinary cue.

Moving to London in 1995, Atkinson helped out at that year's Alternative Miss World, the brainchild competition of artist Andrew Logan, an occasional collaborator and constant inspiration to Atskinson. "He helped me see the rich possibilities of free-form events and a 'just do it' attitude," Atkinson says.

Atkinson has collaborated with designers Ashish, J. Maskrey, and Noki for runway shows, had pieces featured in the Victoria and Albert Museum's Hats: An Anthology by Stephen Jones show, dressed celebrities such as Lady Gaga, Christina Aguilera, Cate Blanchett when she was featured in *Vogue*, Paloma Faith, Lily Allen, Kelis, and Rihanna, as well as Princess Beatrice and Princess Eugenie.

www.piersatkinson.com

Left page: Best before AW12 headpiece photograph by Thomas Cooksey. All images courtesy of Piers Atkinson.

This page:
Isabella hat
Photography: Morgan White

Right page clockwise from top left:
Marlene headpiece
Atropa Belladonna headpiece
Net with multi crystal beauty spots headpiece
Skiap headpiece
Photography: Morgan White

On the following pages:
Left page image:
Agace headpiece
Photography: Leigh Keily
Right page image:
Run for the hills hat
Photography: Leigh Keily

HOLLYWOOD

This page top image:
Shot dupion silk midi-beret
Bottom image:
Handle with care headpiece
Photography: Thomas Cooksey

Left page:
Rosaceae Terribilis headpiece
Photography: Thomas Cooksey

This page clockwise from top left:
Hyper-cherry headpiece
Pink leather and stud headpiece
Felt pillbox with veiling and glitter cherries headpiece
Banana headpiece with dolly
Photography: Leigh Kelly

Left page:
Top image:
Nathan headpiece
Photography: Thomas Cooksey
Bottom image:
Francesca headpiece
Photography: Leigh Kelly

This page:
24-karat gold leaf straw beret with silk flower and veil
Photography: Leigh Keily

Right page:
Pillow headpiece
Illustration by Piers Atkinson

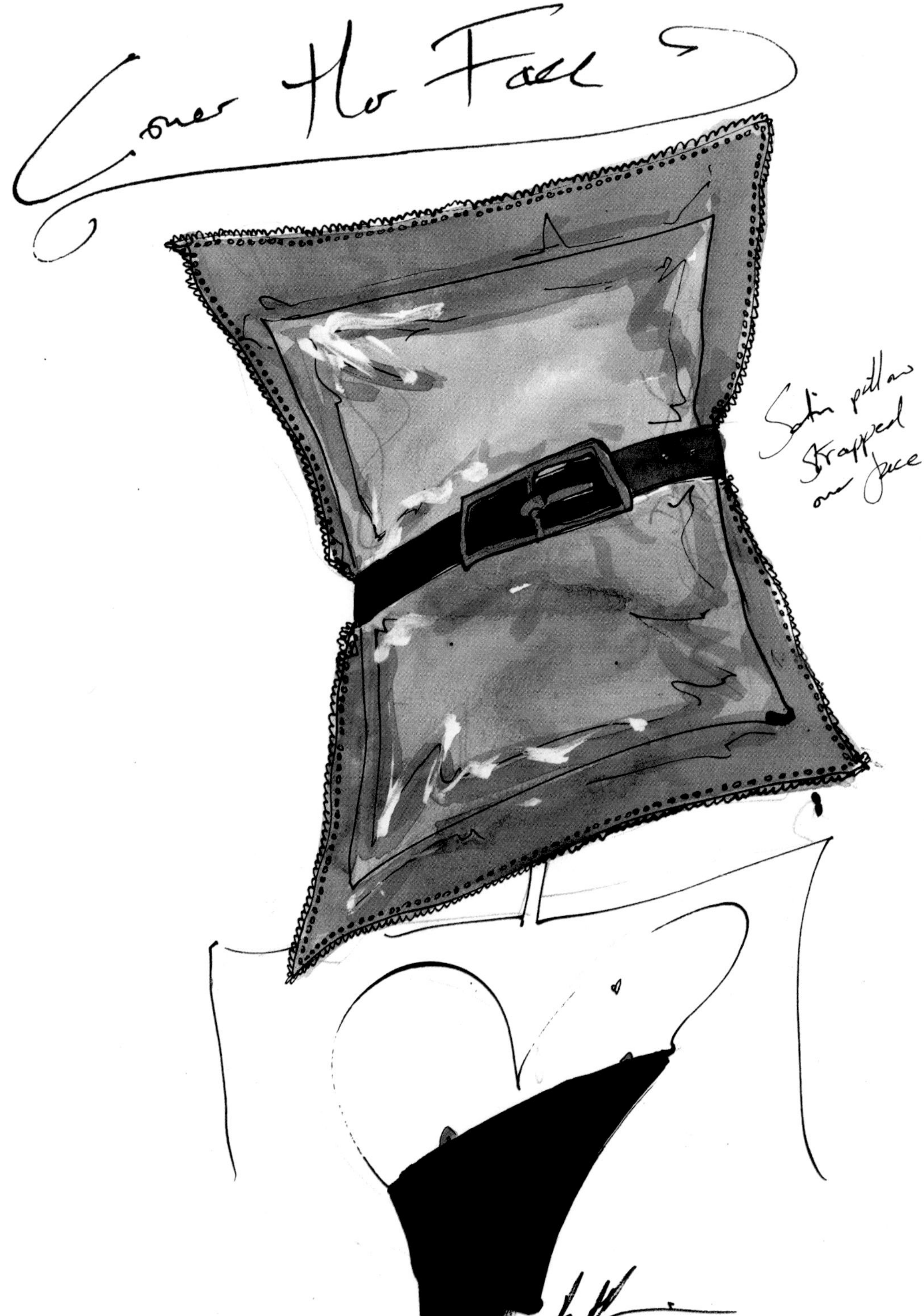

Cover Her Face
Satin pillow
Strapped
over face

IRENE BUSSEMAKER

Irene Bussemaker graduated from Maastricht Academy of Fine Arts in the Netherlands in 1993. While studying there, she apprenticed for Philip Treacy, and this inspired her switch from training to be a fashion designer to training to be a milliner, and over the next few years, Bussemaker was trained by Czech milliner Hanna Hnilicková.

Bussemaker's hats have won several awards, including ones from Chapeau in France, Bollman Headwear Europe, and Tressa AG in the UK. In 2007 she was named Hat Designer of the Year in London and selected as a finalist at International Talent Support's ITS#7 competition sponsored by Diesel in Italy. Her awarded collections were shown in Paris.

Bussemaker's hats are sold at Colette in Paris, Liberty in London, and Alan Journo in Milan. She has collaborated with Dutch fashion designer Iris van Herpen for several seasons, and their specially designed runway pieces have been shown at the London, Paris, and Amsterdam fashion weeks, and during the Mercedes-Benz Dutch Fashion Awards shows.

Bussemaker's work has been featured in international magazines, such as *Vogue*, the French version of *Numéro* magazine, *L'Ófficiel*, *Collezioni*, and *Los Angeles Times Magazine*. Her hats have been requested by stylists Lori Goldstein and Patti Wilson, and worn by celebrities like Christina Hendricks, Milla Jovovich, and Freja Beha Erichsen. They have been photographed by Karl Lagerfeld, Steven Meisel, and Sølve Sundsbø.

www.irenebussemaker.nl

Left page: Photograph of Sonja Wanda by Fotofloor. All images courtesy of Irene Bussemaker.

This page top image:
Irene Bussemaker for Iris van Herpen
Photography: Lotte van den Acker
Bottom image:
Irene Bussemaker for Iris van Herpen
Photography: Michel Zoeter

Left page:
Photography: Tom van Heel and Edel Verzijl

This page top image:
Photograph of Noortje Herlaar by Fotofloor
Bottom image:
Photography: Tom van Heel and Edel Verzijl

Left page:
Photograph of Noortje Herlaar by Fotofloor

This page:
Photography:
Tom van Heel and Edel Verzijl

Right page:
Photograph of Sonja Wanda by Fotofloor

NOEL STEWART

Noel Stewart is a London-based milliner with an international status. Taking inspiration from sources such as contemporary art and architecture and fusing them with historical references, he modernizes millinery with his fresh look at how we dress the head. Before attending the Royal College of Art to do his masters, Stewart had already worked with designers Dai Rees and Stephen Jones. This included time spent as Stephen Jones's assistant at Christian Dior Haute Couture.

Since establishing his own label in 2003, Stewart has designed hats for leading fashion designers, such as Roland Mouret, Marios Schwabb, Roksanda Ilincic, Erdem, Hussein Chalayan, Diesel, Marc by Marc Jacobs, and Oscar de la Renta. His continuing relationship with these designers reflects the importance of his role in the fashion world.

Off the catwalk, Stewart has acquired a loyal fan base. His hats have been worn by the likes of Keira Knightley, Lily Allen, and Beth Ditto, as well Britney Spears and Kylie Minogue on their world tours. They are regularly featured in a number of international versions of *Vogue*, the ones in the UK, Italy, Russia, China, and Japan, as well as in *Harper's Bazaar*, *Dazed & Confused*, *i-D*, *V Magazine*, *LOVE*, *AnOther*, and *10 Magazine*. His work was part of the Stephen Jones anthology of hats exhibition during its showings in Brisbane and New York, and his headpieces are currently stocked in Barneys New York, Hatwoman and I.T in Hong Kong, and Weave Toshi's flagship store in Tokyo.

www.noelstewart.com

Left page: Blown daisy mohican headpiece photograph by Morgan O'Donovan. All images courtesy of Noel Stewart.

This page:
Cocktail hat with angular veil and shards
Photography: Morgan O'Donovan

Right page top image:
Windowpane and parisisal coolie
Bottom image:
Silk and wool crowned hat
Photography: Morgan O'Donovan

This page:
Marbled acrylic and wool petri-topper headpiece
Photography: Morgan O'Donovan

Left page:
Ribboned cityscape headpiece
Photography: Morgan O'Donovan

This page top image:
Linen sun hat with giant gazar tie
Photography: Morgan O'Donovan

Bottom image:
Paint-scraped angular trilby hat
Photography: Morgan O'Donovan

This page top image:
Orange straw coolie
Photography: Morgan O'Donovan

Bottom image:
Hand painted large felt fedora
Photography: Morgan O'Donovan

This page:
Multihat headpiece
Photography: Morgan O'Donovan

Right page:
Gazar and organza crystal headpiece
Photography: Morgan O'Donovan

EMMA YEO

Emma Yeo was born in Brighton, England. In 2009, she obtained a BA in Multimedia Textiles from Loughborough University and an MA in Jewelry Design from Central Saint Martins College of Art and Design in London. Yeo launched her own label in 2010, designing contemporary headwear and accessories that embrace innovation with elegance. The use of fine, laser-cut wood is Yeo's signature style, and her hats demonstrate an unexpected approach to traditional craftsmanship and new technology. The result: fashionable headwear and accessories that challenge the limitations of materials and processes, and complex linear and architectural silhouettes that create subtle intricacies with a refined style. Yeo tailors conventional luxurious and less traditional materials into bespoke, delicate adornments.

Yeo's hats have been featured in *Vogue, Dazed & Confused*, and *The New York Times*. Gaining increasing recognition from the fashion industry, Yeo has been working on commissions by both celebrities and art collectors, and is now attracting enquiries from the film industry. She has participated in several exhibitions in Paris, London, and Italy, and in 2011 her work was featured in London's Selfridges showcase alongside work by Philip Treacy, Alexander McQueen, Hussein Chalayan, and Stephen Jones. Yeo's latest headwear collection "Solitary Motion" was designed in collaboration with Corrie Nielsen's runway show at London Fashion Week.

www.emmayeo.com

Left page: Photograph by Emy Lou. All images courtesy of Emma Yeo.

On these pages:
Photography: Haze Yama at HZV Studios

This page:
Photography: Haze Yama at HZV Studios

Left page:
Photography: Emy Lou

JANE TAYLOR

Jane Taylor earned a degree in embroidery in 2003 and went on to train with London milliners including Queen Elizabeth II's milliner, Marie O'Regan, and work with Bruce Oldfield to create custom headpieces.

Taylor's independent professional career began with her selling her work to private clients and dressing women for the Henley Royal Regatta and the Ascot. She was invited to meet the Queen and Duke of England at a reception for a fashion event and was interviewed by the BBC when they were filming the Ascot race. Her first minor collection was made in Oxfordshire in 2005, the year she opened her own studio in London. Her first major collection was in 2010 and debuted at Harrods.

Drawing inspiration from taxidermy, antiques prints, and couture designs, each of Taylor's headpieces is hand-crafted using an array of delicate feathers, precious silks, distinctive pearls, and Swarovski crystals. Her three collections, bespoke, bridal, and ready-to-wear, are dramatic, ethereal, and theatrical.

Taylor has been featured in magazines such as *Vogue*, *Harper's Bazaar*, *Tatler*, *Elle*, and *InStyle*.

www.janetaylormillinery.com

Left page: Knot straw pillbox photograph by Sarah Jones. All images courtesy of Jane Taylor.

This page left to right:
Black felt comma hat
Fur felt toque hat with felt feathers
Photography: Sarah Jones

Right page:
Rings of Saturn headpiece
Photography: Sarah Jones

This page:
Bird of paradise cocktail hat
Photography: Sarah Jones

Right page:
Bird of paradise cocktail hat
Photography: Geoff Reardon

WILLIAM CHAMBERS

William Chambers earned a degree in Textile Design from the Scottish College of Textiles in 2001. Following graduation, Chambers worked at VV Rouleaux, an eclectic design shop in England, and later moved to Glasgow where he created handmade headpieces and gained in-depth knowledge of the retail industry. In early 2007, Chambers formally studied millinery at Metropolitan University, creating a collection there that was shown to great acclaim at Glasgow Fashion Week. Shortly thereafter, he set up William Chambers Millinery, and received a kick-start to his career when pop star and fashion icon Róisín Murphy wore one of his hats on several occasions during her European tour.

In 2009 the William Chambers Online Hat Shop was launched, allowing customers around the world to purchase Chambers's hats in various colors and sizes via one-click purchasing. The shop has international reach, and its accessibility has resulted in press coverage, most notably from Conde Nast's *Brides* magazine.

In 2010 Chambers was invited to create hats and headpieces for the Dressed to Kilt Fashion Show hosted by Sir Sean Connery in New York City as part of Tartan Week. Other celebrities, such as rock legend Joan Jett who donned his enormous feather headpiece, which resulted in Chambers's name being highlighted in a vast amount of editorials across the globe, are also fans of Chambers. Press such as *Style.com*, *NBC News*, *CBS News*, *New York Post*, *The Telegraph*, *The Sun*, *Metro*, *New Zealand Herald*, and *Hawaii News Now!* have featured his work.

www.williamchambers.co.uk

Left page: Crystal cocktail explosion hat photograph by Niall Walker. All images courtesy of William Chambers.

This page:
Floral twist hat
Photography: Niall Walker

Right page:
Veiled cocktail coolie
Photography: Niall Walker

This page:
Side-fold bow headpiece
Photography: Niall Walker

Left page clockwise from top left:
Copper flower headpiece
Leather pill hat with plastic flowers
Full floral headpiece
Plastic bloomer pill
Photography: Niall Walker

Thanks

I would like to thank all the amazing hat designers and photographers who collaborated with me on this book and helped in the making of it: Alessandra Greco at Philip Treacy, Cornelia de Uphaugh and Maria Eisl at Stephen Jones, Laure Aillagon at Givenchy Haute Couture, Riccardo Tisci, Hèlene Starkman at Christian Dior, Kevind Davies, Laziz Hamani, Olivier Panzo at John Galliano, Myriam Coudoux at Alexander McQueen, Anna Lisa Pirotta at Giorgio Armani, and Kristina Ralph at Giles. A thank-you also to Iris Shih and Julia Abramoff, and a very special thanks to Stephen Jones for writing the foreword of the book. Keep your hats up!